Printed in Great Britain
by Amazon

22561778R00070